S0-CXU-762

# *Responsible Pet Care*

# **Rabbits**

# *Responsible Pet Care*

# Rabbits

**TINA HEARNE**

**Rourke Publications, Inc.**
**Vero Beach, FL 32964**

*A Chocolate Dutch rabbit doe rests with her young. Rabbits are essentially outdoor animals and should not be confined indoors.*

## Library of Congress Cataloging-in-Publication Data

Hearne, Tina.
  Rabbits/by Tina Hearne.

      p. cm - (Responsible pet care)
  Includes index.
  Summary: Examines the different varieties of rabbits and describes how they may be housed, exercised, handled, fed, cleaned, and bred.
  ISBN 0-86625-187-1
  1. Rabbits - Juvenile literature. [1. Rabbits.] I. Title.
II. Series.
SF453.2.H45 1989
636'.932'2-dc19          88-37901
                              CIP
  PRINTED IN THE USA        AC

# CONTENTS

# Why Choose A Rabbit?

The rabbit is a popular and successful pet. After many years of intensive breeding programs, a wide range of suitable pets is available. There are rabbits as different as the Angora, the Californian, the Dutch, and the Lop-eared.

Most rabbits soon become tame if regularly groomed and handled from an early age. The smallest dwarf varieties are very docile and easy to handle. Rabbits are also capable of developing strong personalities of their own, particularly if they live in a stimulating environment and do not become lethargic with boredom. They can be very rewarding pets to keep and are always interesting to watch.

Generally healthy and hardy, rabbits are quite easy to care for, feeding on an entirely **herbivorous diet**. They are essentially outdoor animals, not suitable for keeping indoors. They are definitely not a pet for those who live in an apartment. Any attempt to keep a rabbit closely confined in a restricted space would be cruel.

*The Lop, with its exaggerated ears, is one of the fancy rabbit breeds created for the show bench.*

*The Lilac Californian rabbit is a twentieth century American variety bred originally for meat. It is a big, beautiful white rabbit with dark points, like the Himalayan rabbit or the Siamese cat.*

Good accommodations are vital to successful rabbit keeping. They quickly become bored and frustrated with inadequate housing conditions. Rabbits need a roomy, secure hutch and an exercise area that is safely enclosed. They need opportunity to gnaw and to burrow. Being underground animals that in the wild live in a network of underground burrows, they must have access to a secluded spot where they can remain out of sight if they wish.

# Varieties

Once thought to be rodents, rabbits are now classed as *Lagomorphs*, which means "shaped like the hare." The colors of domestic rabbits include black, white, blue, lilac, fawn, chocolate, tan, orange, red, havana, and several shades of gray. Rabbits with a single, uniform color are **self-colored**. **Broken-colored** rabbits have more than one color. The separation of the colors may be obvious, as in a tortoiseshell or Himalayan rabbit, which has dark points like a Siamese cat. In other breeds, such as the Chinchilla, the rabbit's coat looks silver. It is made up of white guard hairs evenly spaced between the dark underhair.

Rabbit breeds are classified according to coat type. The normal breeds have coats similar in length and texture to those of the wild rabbit. Normal breeds include the Argentés, Beverens, Lilacs, and the Siberians. The Chinchilla, Sable, and Silver Fox are also normal breeds. Their coats are meant to imitate those of the animals whose names they bear.

*Small and compact, the Netherland Dwarfs have proved themselves fine pets. This juvenile, or kitten, has the markings of the Himalayan.*

*The coat of this young chinchilla rabbit is soft and lovely with mottled coloring. It resembles the fur of the South American chinchilla, after which it is named. The chinchilla rabbit was originally bred for its fur.*

The fancy breeds are novelty breeds, many of them developed primarily for the show bench. They include the Angora, Belgian Hare, English, Flemish Giant, Harlequin, Himalayan, Lop-eared, Magpie, Polish Dwarf, and Netherland breeds.

All these variations of color, ears, markings, and size have been bred from **mutations**. The Rex and Satin breeds are also the result of mutation. Rexes have dense, short hair, but no long guard hairs, giving a characteristic coat type. The Satins, an American breed, have fur that rolls back, giving this breed its characteristic sheen.

# The Hutch

A homemade hutch is often the best: strong, secure, and spacious. Two small or medium-sized rabbits will need a hutch at least five feet long. There should be two feet of headroom, and two feet of depth in the hutch.

Divide the interior into two communicating compartments: one for daytime; the other for night. Design the hutch so that the whole front opens on hinges, like two doors. The day compartment needs a door of wire mesh, for ventilation and visibility. The sleeping quarters need a solid door for privacy and security. Some owners have an extra shutter to use over the wire mesh at night.

Both compartments should have a generous supply of straw or shredded paper on the floor to absorb urine. Do not use newspaper because the ink can be harmful to rabbits if swallowed. In addition, the sleeping quarters need plenty of clean bedding material, such as straw, according to temperature. In very cold weather, the rabbits will need to snuggle into a complete ball of straw at night.

*This pet rabbit is in the night-time section of its hutch. The thick layer of straw on the floor absorbs urine.*

*A New Zealand white rabbit and her crossbred litter inhabit this two-compartment, well designed hutch. It can be cleaned easily by raking all the soiled floor litter forward and replacing it with a fresh layer. Hay is available from a hay rack to prevent its being constantly stepped on.*

Rabbits suffer in both heat and cold. Any hutch, however well built, will not be very well insulated. You should be prepared to vary the position of the hutch according to the season. If you live in an area where it snows during the winter, for example, you will have to move the hutch into the shelter of a shed or garage. In hot weather, it must stand in the shade.

# The Exercise Ark

An exercise ark is meant to be portable and should be built with this in mind. The most common design begins with a triangular framework, covered with wire mesh. It should be about five feet long, two feet deep, and two feet tall at its highest point. Wire mesh on the base, as well as on the sides, prevents burrowing and keeps the rabbits safe. One end can be roofed over to provide shelter.

The exercise ark has two very important uses. As its name suggests, the ark gives pet rabbits a safe place, other than the hutch, to exercise. It can be moved from place to place, in or out of the sun, according to the rabbits' needs at the time. Having an exercise ark helps to keep the hutch dry and clean. When rabbits are shut in the hutch for long periods, the hutch quickly becomes damp and smelly. An ark provides rabbits with some exercise and a change of scene.

*The exercise ark is portable enough to be moved from place to place, according to the vegetation and the weather. It is not sturdy enough to be used as permanent housing, but used together with a good hutch, it provides the rabbit with interest, variety, and natural grazing.*

*A period of freedom, preferably all day, out of the hutch gives rabbits a much better quality of life. A securely fenced area is useful, but they eventually eat all the vegetation and it becomes a bare patch.*

An ark can also be used as a grazing pen. Rabbits are by nature grazing animals. Like all **herbivores**, they spend a great deal of their time feeding. Provided the spaces between the mesh on the base of the ark are wide enough to allow vegetation to poke through, the ark allows the rabbits to graze naturally on grass and suitable wild plants. Always be careful to avoid any vegetation that may have been sprayed with weed killer.

# Exercise

Responsible pet owners understand that rabbits are very energetic creatures and cannot be happy if too closely confined. The problem, always, is to find ways of keeping them safe while allowing adequate exercise.

The exercise ark is recommended, but there are other options. Rabbits are companionable animals. They will often be content to spend some time in the company of their owner in, for example, a garage or shed. There they can enjoy some free play. Many owners also allow their rabbits some freedom in the house. In either case, be watchful. Rabbits love to gnaw and may do damage by gnawing through cables.

A safer way to provide opportunity for exercise is to build a larger enclosure around the hutch. During the day, the hutch is opened up and the rabbits are given the run of the whole area. A ramp can be put in front of the open hutch to provide safe access. Even without a ramp, rabbits can climb and jump to and from their hutch.

*The rabbit, with its well developed hind legs, is an active animal, able to cover large distances in the wild. In captivity, providing sufficient opportunity for exercise is one of the main duties of the responsible pet owner.*

*Rabbits can be allowed out of the hutch to play with their owners, but never leave them out of the hutch without being present to supervise — and never leave them with other animals. Some dogs might see a rabbit as ready prey.*

The enclosure should be at least three feet high for safety. The secret of keeping rabbits safe in the enclosure is to sink the fencing below the surface of the ground. Any rabbits who attempt to burrow under the fence will be foiled.

The earth in an enclosure quickly becomes bare. Compensate for that by sometimes putting the rabbits in their exercise ark in places where there is suitable vegetation.

# Handling

How should you pick up a rabbit? Steady the rabbit by holding the skin at the back of the neck with one hand, and put your other hand under the rabbit's body. When you lift up, the weight of the animal is supported from beneath.

Rabbits are far too heavy to be picked up by the ears or by the scruff of the neck. When adult rabbits pick up their young that way, they are handling only very light animals.

Large breeds, those that weigh as much as twelve pounds, can be hard to handle. This is one reason that smaller breeds, such as the dwarf rabbits, the Dutch, or the English, are often recommended as pets. No matter which breed you have, handle your rabbits frequently if you want them to become tame. When several people are going to be handling the same rabbit, it helps to make the rabbit **tractable** if you all agree to use the same method of lifting. In this way the rabbit knows what to expect and how to respond.

Most rabbits, and in particular the dwarf varieties such as you see here, become very tame and tractable in time. Handle them frequently from a young age, but be gentle and support their weight in your arms.

*Never pick up a rabbit by its ears. Instead, hold the skin at the back of the neck, and slide the other hand under the body to support the rabbit's weight.*

Sometimes a rabbit will scratch you accidentally. This may happen just as it is being returned to the hutch. The rabbit kicks out with its strong back legs to reach the hutch quickly. Expert handlers avoid being kicked or scratched in this way by returning the rabbit to the hutch with the rabbit facing backwards. That way, the strong back legs can do no harm.

17

# Feeding

Most rabbits enjoy and thrive on one basic meal a day as long as it is supplemented with plenty of hay, fresh vegetable matter, fresh grazing, a mineral lick, and clean drinking water.

A mixture of grains, bran, and rabbit pellets makes a good meal. Rabbit mixtures that contain these ingredients are available in pet stores. If you mix your own, you can provide the grain in the form of wholemeal bread. To make the food into a mash, add a little hot water or hot milk.

Wild rabbits are entirely herbivorous after the age of suckling. Many pet rabbits, particularly breeding females, benefit from being given some milk. Keep in mind that milk quickly turns sour in warm climates.

*The rabbit's front incisor teeth grow continuously, as in other gnawing animals, such as the beaver. In captivity, there is a danger that these teeth may become overgrown and eventually force apart the jaws so that the animal can no longer feed. Hard food and pieces of wood to gnaw on will keep the teeth short and sharp.*

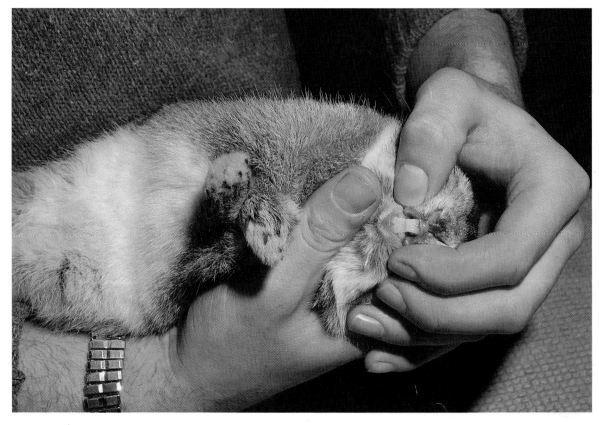

*These young rabbits are feeding on pellet food in their hutch. Pellet food is very convenient, but it does not occupy the rabbits for long. As grazing animals, they are better occupied if given some hard food, such as root vegetables, to supplement their pellet diet.*

Some rabbits prefer dry food rather than a mash. Feed them a commercial mixture, wholemeal bread baked hard, or pellets. Pellets are convenient and nutritious, but rabbits eat them too quickly. Herbivores are used to grazing for their meals, which keeps them occupied while feeding. Pellets do not occupy a rabbit's time, and many rabbits eat too many pellets and become fat. Overcome this problem by providing fresh vegetables, particularly hard root vegetables for the rabbits to gnaw.

Gnawing hard food helps rabbits in another way. It wears down the front **incisor teeth** that grow continuously and can eventually interfere with proper feeding.

All rabbits, especially those fed mainly on pellets, must be given fresh drinking water every day.

# Cleaning And Grooming

Rabbits can be a lot of work for their owners. If you want to keep rabbits, cleaning their hutch must be one of your top priorities. The floor litter may need replacing as often as every day.

Two things will make your job easier. First, keep the rabbits out of the hutch for as long as possible during the day, providing they are comfortable. Let them use either the enclosure, or an exercise ark. Second, use a highly absorbent floor litter in the hutch to soak up urine. Alternatively, use washable trays on the hutch floor, beneath the litter. Once a week, clean the hutch thoroughly. Scrape it out and, if necessary, scrub, rinse, and dry it before returning the rabbits. Remember that animals do not normally soil their bedding. That should not need replacing. Although it is important to keep your rabbits in clean accommodations, do not disturb them unduly.

*Grooming time is valuable, because it gives the owner a fine opportunity to observe a rabbit closely. Pay attention to the ears, eyes, and claws, and note if there are any parasites in the coat or bald patches that need veterinary attention.*

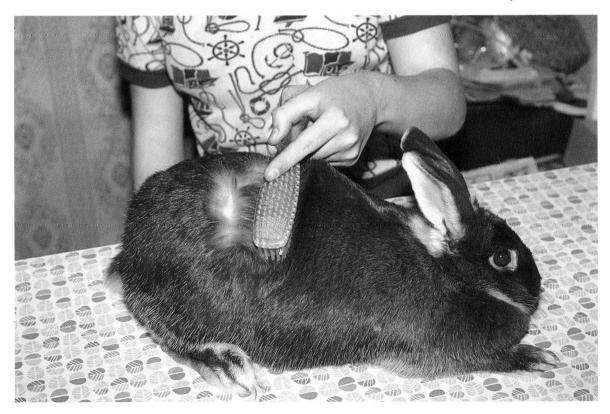

*The Angora is the breed that cannot groom itself. Its wool coat, quite unlike that of any other breed of rabbit, needs daily grooming.*

Most rabbits are able to groom themselves, but benefit if their coat is brushed once a week. Brushing cleans the skin. It removes loose hairs and small pieces of leaf and twig which cling to the coat. The breed which cannot groom itself is the Angora. Its wool coat, quite unlike that of any other breed, can become tangled unless groomed daily, and clipped regularly.

Grooming time is valuable. It gives responsible pet owners the chance to observe their rabbits. Pay particular attention to the ears, eyes, and claws. Notice whether there are any **parasites.** Is there any condition, such as bald patches in the coat, needing attention or veterinary treatment?

21

# Breeding

Male rabbits are called bucks; females are does. A buck and doe cannot be housed together for life. The buck is not a good family animal, and the strain of constant breeding would exhaust the doe.

Breeders house their bucks separately and introduce a pair on neutral ground for mating. If a mating is successful the doe should **kindle**, or have a **litter**, approximately 31 days later. She is a very fine mother, and all the responsibility of rearing the litter falls on her. Three weeks or so after mating, provide her with hay to construct her nest. The hutch should be adapted by the introduction of a shelf where she can sometimes relax away from her demanding babies, once they are born. The doe will need a good quality diet, and far more food than usual – perhaps twice the normal amount during pregnancy, and even three times the normal amount when suckling her litter.

*Three weeks after mating, provide the doe with hay from which to construct her nest. The young will be born after a pregnancy of approximately thirty-one days.*

*Young rabbits, called kittens, are weaned between six and eight weeks of age. Breeding is exhausting, and the doe needs a rest between pregnancies.*

After raising her young, the doe needs a period of rest. Repeated pregnancies and the strain of suckling can quickly exhaust her. Because rabbits are so prolific, breeding them is not difficult, but it can soon become unmanageable because of the numbers of young that may be produced. Everyone who plans to breed rabbits should join the American Rabbit Breeders Association (P.O. Box 426, Bloomington, IL 61702). Write to them for information; you will benefit from the knowledge and support they can provide.

# The Young

Newborn rabbits are called kittens. An average litter will contain about six or eight young rabbits. At first the kittens are very undeveloped. In the wild they would remain unseen in the underground nest for about three weeks. In captivity, they should also remain unseen for about the same length of time. Any undue interference, particularly at first, may turn the doe against them. It is not unknown for young rabbits to be killed by an over-anxious doe whose nest has been disturbed. Do not give in to the temptation to look at the kittens too soon.

*This young tortoiseshell rabbit is probably two weeks old. Kittens emerge from the nest at about three weeks of age.*

*Kittens can live together to the age of about ten weeks. By then they must be separated. The males need to live independently; a group of females may remain together for life.*

When the young emerge from the nest at three weeks, their hair will have grown, their eyes will have opened, and they will begin to nibble at solid food, such as hay, or take some wholemeal bread soaked in milk.

The kittens remain suckling until six or eight weeks of age. By ten weeks, they should be separated. Keeping the young together too long encourages mating between them, which is unwise with such immature animals. Keeping males together after the age of three months leads to serious fighting.

When possible, house two or more rabbits together for company. Two or more females will live peaceably together, although any pregnant female must be given her own hutch. Because males are aggressive with each other, they need to be housed individually for life to avoid fighting.

# Ailments

A common disease among pet rabbits is snuffles, which can lead to pneumonia. Snuffles is similar to the common cold in man. It is highly infectious, so isolate any rabbit with symptoms of sneezing, noisy breathing, or runny nose. Prompt veterinary treatment is recommended.

Rabbits are also prey to several parasites. Fleas cause them to scratch furiously. Fleas cluster in the fur, especially around the neck, and their droppings show up as dark spots in the fur. Fleas breed in the host animal's bedding, not in the rabbit's coat. Thoroughly clean the hutch, and change all the floor litter and bedding. Use an insecticide flea powder.

The dreadful rabbit disease, *Myxomatosis*, is carried by the rabbit flea. This disease destroys whole populations of wild rabbits, but it is seldom a threat to pet ones. If there is any risk of contact, a vaccine is available from your veterinarian.

*This wild rabbit has the dreaded disease, Myxomatosis. This disease kills whole populations of wild rabbits but seldom affects pet ones. If there is any danger of a pet rabbit being infected by contact with the wild rabbit population, seek immediate veterinary advice. A vaccine is available.*

*Domestic rabbits: (left to right) Yellow, Black, and Agouti Dutch, in show condition.*

Lice may also attack the rabbit. They leave white eggs, called nits, in the rabbit's fur. Use an insecticide lice powder for a period to kill off all the generations of an infestation. Seek veterinary help if necessary.

Mites can cause rabbits great pain, irritation, and distress. Some mites burrow beneath the skin, causing skin mange. There are also mites that cause ear canker. Any infestation of mites requires prompt veterinary treatment.

Caring for a sick rabbit is a fundamental responsibility of pet keeping. Understand, before you get a rabbit, that at some time veterinary fees are likely to be incurred.

# Health And Longevity

Rabbits are one of the most adaptable and successful animals on earth. They are naturally healthy and hardy. Signs of health include a good coat, free of parasites and bare patches. Healthy skin is clean, with no sores or symptoms of irritation. The eyes should be clear and bright. The inside of the ears should be clean, without deposits such as the brown matter that indicates the presence of ear mites. Normal breathing is quiet and even. Normal droppings are dry and hold their shape.

The healthy rabbit is alert and watchful. Periods of activity such as grazing, gnawing, and burrowing are followed by quiet periods when the rabbit is resting. In the wild, rabbits are seen to be far more active at night. They are mainly **nocturnal**, or **crepuscular**. In captivity, most have adapted to a **diurnal** life style. As some still retain the wild instinct to be active at night, allow your rabbits to select the time of day when they rest, and leave them undisturbed.

*A rabbit is likely to live for six or eight years. Many reach ten years or more.*

*Like all pet animals, rabbits are likely to remain in good health throughout their life if kept in good accommodations and fed a nutritious diet. Their standard of life affects their longevity.*

Caged animals, including rabbits, remain in better health if their accommodation is maintained at a high standard and if their diet is varied and nutritious. Rabbits, like so many other small animals, have very poor powers of recuperation. Once they fall ill, they deteriorate rapidly. Only prompt and effective medical attention will save them.

In good health, rabbits may be expected to live for at least six to eight years. Many survive for ten years or even longer.

# GLOSSARY

Broken-colored

A rabbit with a coat of two or more colors, such as black and white.

Crepuscular

Active at dawn and at dusk.

Diurnal

Active during the day.

Herbivores

Animals that feed entirely on plant matter.

Herbivorous diet

A diet consisting entirely of vegetable matter, in contrast to a carnivorous diet (of animal products), and an omnivorous diet (a mixture of plant and animal foods).

Incisor teeth

A rabbit's two front teeth, which grow continuously.

Kindle

To have a litter of baby rabbits.

Litter

The group of offspring that a rabbit gives birth to at one time.

Mutation

A genetic change that is passed on to the next generation.

Parasites

Fleas and other organisms that live on the blood of other animals.

Nocturnal

Active at night.

Self-colored

A rabbit that is a solid color, such as all-white or all-black.

Tractable

Docile and easily handled.

# INDEX

We would like to thank and acknowledge the following people for the use of their photographs and transparencies:

| | |
|---|---|
| Cover | Jane Burton/Bruce Coleman Ltd |
| Title Page | Jane Burton/Bruce Coleman Ltd |
| P. 6/7 | Jane Burton/Bruce Coleman Ltd<br>Ardea London Ltd |
| P. 8/9 | Aquila Photographics Ltd |
| P. 10/11 | Sally Anne Thompson/Animal Photography<br>Sally Anne Thompson/RSPCA |
| P. 12/13 | Jane Burton/Bruce Coleman Ltd<br>RSPCA |
| P. 14/15 | Ardea London Ltd<br>Hans Reinhard/Bruce Coleman Ltd |
| P. 16/17 | Sally Anne Thompson/Animal Photography<br>Hans Reinhard/Bruce Coleman Ltd |
| P. 18/19 | Aquila Photographics Ltd<br>Jane Burton/Bruce Coleman Ltd |
| P. 20/21 | Marc Henrie ASC<br>Jane Burton/Bruce Coleman Ltd |
| P. 22/23 | Hans Reinhard/Bruce Coleman Ltd |
| P. 24/25 | Jane Burton/Bruce Coleman Ltd<br>Sally Anne Thompson/Animal Photography Ltd |
| P. 26/27 | Gordon Langsbury/Bruce Coleman Ltd<br>Jane Burton/Bruce Coleman Ltd |
| P. 28/29 | Jane Burton/Bruce Coleman Ltd |